You Can Win Being You!

Success Is A Process, Not An Event

4th Edition

Mills Carnell Rodgers II

DEDICATION

I dedicate this book to my family for the insights and inspiration to pursue this project. I love you!

You Can Win Being You!

CONTENTS

You Can Win Being You!

INTRODUCTION

How many of you have seen the commercials and infomercials for exercise equipment and programs? Have you noticed that the people in these advertisements generally appear to be in great shape? They always seem to have a smile on their face. They also seem to be using the equipment or program with ease, right? If someone didn't know any better, it would seem as though improving our physiques is a leisurely undertaking. However, most of us know this is not the case! Improving our bodies and conditioning is a demanding task which can cause you some discomfort and pain along the way. There will be sweat and strain. It is certainly not as glamorous as the ads make it out to be!

The same principles that apply to changing our physique apply to improving ourselves, whether it is our education, careers, starting a business, or simply getting our lives together. Whatever you are trying to do, you will likely experience some pain & strain along the way. Pain may come from a lack of resources. The amount of sacrifice and effort needed can generate stress. Setbacks can cause emotional pain. This is simply all part of the process. Our bodies require us to strain and sweat in order to reach a higher level of conditioning and health. There is no way around it. Even though it is a great sacrifice, it is well worth it for the improvements to our health. Well, guess what? Just like our bodies, we must go through pains in order to reach our goals. It is not easy! Sometimes you will want to quit. That is normal. Ask anyone who has sought to do things on a higher level; many will tell you that they considered throwing in the towel along the way. However, they will all tell you this: THE KEY IS NOT TO QUIT! It takes a lot for all of us, including myself, to stay encouraged and reach the next level. The grind is worth it in the end. The purpose of this book is to provide insights, strategies, and, more importantly, hope, in helping you reach the level of success you are seeking to attain!

Chapter 1

IT STARTS WITH YOU!

(SELF EMPOWERMENT)

Do you desire to better yourself or situation? It all starts with **YOU**. **YOU** must believe in yourself. **YOU** have to believe what you are doing is going to work. **YOU** must believe, through your efforts, opportunities will arise that are **FOR YOU**. Yes, **YOU CAN WIN BEING YOU!!** Trying to better yourself or situation is never easy. It always requires leaving our comfort zone. It involves the risk of failure. I once heard someone say to be exceptional you must be the exception.

I know, you are probably thinking about your own unique situation. You're probably saying to yourself, "I've heard all this stuff before, but my situation is different...it isn't that simple." Trust me, I am VERY aware that we all experience challenging circumstances of varying degrees. I taught for 15 years in public

3

schools and saw many issues. I have also experienced my own.

I'll be honest, our environment can influence our situations, no matter how much we try not to let it. If you're a student, it could be issues at home with parents, abuse, or poverty, for example. As an adult, it could be marital, financial, or child related. No doubt, all these issues present us with challenges and are not easy to overcome. However, the reality is that we must take the initiative to make things better. Especially as a mature person, no one can make your situation better for you than you. You may feel like life isn't always fair when you compare yourself to others. That is understandable. I'll raise my hand; I am guilty of that myself. But then I realize that someone could compare themselves to me and feel the same way.

The first step in achieving success is understanding that the person you see in the mirror is the one responsible for the **SHAPE** you are in! When I say SHAPE, I don't mean physical fitness (well, I guess I could mean that also). **SHAPE**, in my world, means the following:

- **S**- Success
- **H**- Happiness
- **A- ATTITUDE**
- **P**- Progress
- **E**- Effort

Everything about the SHAPE you're in centers on your attitude, which is why it is in caps and bolded. Attitude is everything! If you can have a positive resilient attitude, it will impact the other aspects of SHAPE in the same way: your success, happiness, progress, and effort. I think we all have an idea of what those terms mean, so I'm not going to insult your intelligence by explaining them. **Now, I'm not saying it is going to be easy!** Some of us come from horrible situations. I have seen people who grew up homeless, abused, had neglectful parents, and those who have witnessed horrific events. If this is you, it is ok to get professional help coping with these experiences.

The reality is we must make a choice to be positive, regardless of our situation. Some situations, like I mentioned, are traumatizing. We often need help to get to the point of being able to choose being positive. Once you make the choice to be positive, there will be times you get discouraged. Man, I wish I could promise you it won't happen, but I would be lying if I did. There are so many things that can happen daily that will frustrate you. Some are rather trivial; some are very serious. Positive people experience emotions just like everyone else. The key is controlling what you can control and having realistic goals you can shoot for. I will be talking more about these ideas in later chapters.

In the meantime, I have included some tips which take SHAPE into account. We can apply these so that we have the proper mindset needed to stay on that sometimes rocky, but rewarding, path of self-improvement.

1. **Believe In YOU.** First and foremost, you must believe that what you are doing is going to result in success in some form or fashion. You can't rely on others to always spur you into action. It is great to have a support system, but it is meaningless if you don't believe in yourself. Others can encourage, but you have to act. Everything starts and ends with you!

2. **Tune out the Noise.** Many people will not understand. Some will flatly say you can't do it. Some will think you are crazy. Some will ask why would you want to make yourself so much trouble, why not just go with the status quo? Get used to hearing it. You are going against the grain. It is likely that most people are not doing what you are trying to do, whether it's starting a business, improving your health, growing spiritually, etc. It's only natural that some may not throw their full support behind you. Expect it and accept it.

3. **Keep an Open Mind.** Do your research. Continue to learn about the area you are seeking to improve upon. We are in an age where we have an ability to access limitless information at our fingertips. There are usually several ways to accomplish a goal and, through your own research and observation, you may find your own way of doing it that works well for your situation.

4. **Have a positive attitude.** You must believe in what you are doing. You must have a can-do attitude. The glass is half full, not half empty. Being positive doesn't mean you are unaware of challenges or that bad things won't happen to you. You will have setbacks. Exceptional people don't dwell on their setbacks or do much complaining.

5. **Find your talent/passion.** Unfortunately, talent in our culture seems to always be equated to athletics or entertainment, especially for our youth. There are many talents outside of those areas, such as being a leader, educating, and trade skills, to name a few. Many talents/passions take time to discover and develop; we may not have a clue what our talents are until we are far into adulthood.

6. **Work hard.** You will put in the work if you are passionate about what you are attempting to accomplish.

7. **Faith.** Believe in your higher power & yourself. It will likely take a belief in something outside of yourself to accomplish your goals.

Remember, you bring something unique to this world. Some will say that there are already a lot of people doing what you are attempting to do. So what!! When I look at the busy street nearby in my city, I see 5 fast food restaurants that sell burgers within approximately 1 mile of each other. And they are all profitable. Do you know what that tells me? There is always room for your own unique approach, what you bring to the table. Empower yourself by realizing you can make your goals a reality!

SUMMARY: Understanding the power you have, your beliefs, and who you are, is the catalyst to navigate your road to success. Circumstances can have an influence on our actions but, ultimately, we all must make choices on how we will respond to situations and how we will act. NO ONE else can do this for you!

ACTION PLAN: Taking action is key to becoming empowered. What are two positive habits you can acquire, in the short term, to increase your self-confidence so that you can take more responsibility and become empowered?

Chapter 2

THE START OF A NEW SEASON

(UNDERSTANDING THE CHALLENGE)

The beginning of September signals the start of one of our country's favorite past times …. football season! Over the years, I have seen how sports provides such great analogies for life in general. Just like the start of a sports season, our lives can be broken down into seasons: a new year, the start of a new job, a new relationship, a new school year, etc. The examples are endless.

There are many lessons that can be learned in equating the start of the football season to the various seasons and cycles in our lives. What follows is a list of situations that a football team encounters during a typical season that equates to what we experience in our lives:

1. **Importance of preparation.** Every team has prepared by learning and training during the offseason. Each team has spent many hours doing conditioning and learning plays. A lack of preparation will definitely ensure that the team will be unsuccessful. Same with us on an individual level. We cannot take advantage of an opportunity if we are unprepared mentally, physically, emotionally, etc. We must commit ourselves to learning and improvement. If we want to excel at our goals, we must work on mastering ourselves through self-discipline and accountability.

2. **Losing (disappointment).** Most teams will lose at least once. It is rare that a team makes it through a season undefeated. Several years ago, the New York Giants won the Super Bowl having lost half of their regular season games. In life, we will suffer disappointments, but the good news is that, like the New York Giants, we do not need to be close to perfect to succeed at our goals. More importantly, we must develop the mental stamina to deal with the disappointments which may arise.

3. **Injuries (unexpected challenges).** Teams will have key players that get injured. It's a kind of paradox. No one hopes for this to happen, but it is expected. Those

teams that have good systems in place always seem to suffer less of an impact when this happens. This relates to preparation and foresight. Disclaimer: There are things that happen to us, just like an injury to a key player on a team, which can derail a whole season: health issues, natural disasters, etc. Let's be honest, we are resilient; we can recover from many things that happen to us, but it can be extremely challenging in terms of effort, time, and our emotions. We want to focus on things within our circle of control. This is where preparation helps (See number 1).

4. **One Game at a Time (the process).** A team must focus on winning the game at hand, not the game that is 3 weeks from now or the championship. Winning the game at hand puts the team closer to its goal of making the playoffs or winning a title. Same with us on an individual level. We must focus on the steps to accomplishing our goal as opposed to the actual goal itself. It is great to dream big, but in general, it is not very helpful in accomplishing the goal. Mastering certain skills and strategies are the keys to accomplishment. A great example for this concept is weight loss. A common New Year's resolution is to lose ___ lbs. by summertime. There is absolutely nothing wrong with setting this goal. However, the

focus has to be more on "how" you will reach that goal and "what" you will do. What is your plan for dieting? Is it reasonable? What is your exercise plan? The consistency in implementation will help you reach your goal more than simply creating a goal.

While we're talking about consistency in our season, let's touch on the concept of effort. How many times have you heard someone say the following?

"Do your best!"
"Give 100%!"
"You must give it your all, all of the time!"

I'm sure you have heard those clichés numerous times; we should be following them, right? While they are meant to be encouraging, they can also be discouraging. You might be thinking to yourself, "How is that?" Well, here is the reality. We have all watched sporting events in which a team or athlete may simply have a bad day, despite their best efforts, for reasons that are often unknown to the general public. The same can apply to us in our lives. Your "100%" can vary from day to day, based on a few factors. You may have a "good night's rest, I'm in love, pay day, absolutely best day 100%." Or you may have a "sick/injured, slept 2 hours last night, car won't start, bad day 100%." If you think that you have to be at your "best day 100%" every day, you are likely setting yourself up for disappointment. Your best day does not occur every day, so for you to perform at the "100%" of your best day, every day, is unrealistic and self-defeating. However, you can realistically perform at 100% everyday based on how you are feeling or what you are going through for THAT PARTICULAR DAY! You can be the best you can be for that situation. It may not be your all-time best, but it is your best for that moment! We all have to deal with adversity in our lives, just like a team has to deal with adversity during a season. Yet, we can all come out of it as champions!

SUMMARY: Whatever goal or dream you pursue; you will experience highs and lows. The lessons we learn from our disappointments can lead to growth. While your 100% best can vary from day to day based on a few factors, you can still give your best every day. The key is to stay reasonably consistent in our habits to accomplish our goals.

ACTION PLAN: When chasing your dreams/goals, you will inevitably have bad days. What are some strategies that you can use to push through?

Chapter 3

GOOD THINGS ARE SUPPOSED
TO HAPPEN TO ME!

(THE POWER OF MINDSET)

Les Brown is my absolute favorite motivational speaker. I see him as the Michael Jordan of speakers. His versatility and ability to relate to a variety of audiences is unmatched, in my opinion. He is the G.O.A.T. (Greatest Of All Time). Anyhow, enough of my motivational speaking man crush on Les Brown.

One day, I was watching a motivational video of Les Brown on YouTube. YouTube is such an awesome resource; I wish it was around back in the day when I was coming up. Anyway, in the video, Mr. Brown instructed the audience to say, "Good things are supposed to happen to me." He recommended that the audience say this to themselves daily.

Brown went on to say we tend to anticipate bad things happening to us, so we need to affirm the positive. It got me to thinking: do we really expect bad things to happen to us? Or do we expect that good things will NOT happen for us? I don't think we expect tragedy to occur in our lives, but we don't expect to have things go our way. We don't expect to get "lucky." There is a perverted comfort in this approach to our mindset. If you condition yourself not to expect a lot out of life, I guess you can avoid disappointment. Disappointment is a difficult pill to swallow. No one enjoys disappointment. After suffering repeated disappointments, we tend to want to avoid it at all costs. That is why so many people, unfortunately, turn to substances to avoid dealing with the pain of past and present disappointments. Of course, that isn't the answer.

So yes, we may not expect tragic things to happen, but we don't expect good things to happen as a way of guarding against disappointment. The unfortunate thing about this type of mental conditioning is that it undermines ambition and hope. I'm sure most of you have heard that if you don't expect to succeed at something, you likely won't. If you don't have the expectation, it is unlikely that you will put forth the required effort and persistence needed. You've never heard an athlete, after winning a game, title, etc., say that they didn't expect or deserve to win. They almost always say they believed in themselves, even if no one else did. It all starts with a belief.

In his speech, Les Brown was emphasizing the importance of being positive, making affirmations. Affirmations are designed to change our subconscious thoughts by constantly referring to them in our conscious minds. Our subconscious impacts us in ways we are unaware of. We tend to have thought patterns and experiences in our past which, if we are not aware, can undermine our conscious efforts to do better in the present. By constantly affirming the positive, the goal is to change our inner dialogue. What we hear repeatedly tends to impact us. Think about it. How many of us remember the words to songs we hear constantly on the radio, even if we don't like it?!?

A positive example I have of this was in my classroom. Sometimes I would play motivational speeches in the background as students work independently. One of the students shared with me that she was studying one night and was falling asleep; however, she recalled one of the speeches I played in class that said you have to push through when you feel like giving up. It prompted her to resume studying! Hearing her say that was like music to my ears; it encouraged me to keep playing those speeches.

So, what happens when we start to internalize the message that "good things are supposed to happen to me?" Does that mean everything we pursue will happen? Of course not! Does it mean that you won't be disappointed? Absolutely not! However, the benefit is that you start to perceive the world differently. Because you are perceiving the world positively, you start to recognize your blessings. You take on an attitude of gratitude! And there is something about being grateful. It hasn't been proven scientifically (yet), but when you are sincerely thankful, you tend to attract more blessings and positivity in our lives.

I cannot emphasize enough that having a positive mindset does not mean things will always great or fair. I will be honest. Many of us, including myself, have experienced being treated unfairly because of gender, race, country of origin, and sexuality, among many other reasons. This treatment is typically grounded in stereotypes and cultural conditioning. Trust me, I understand how it is unfair and can make one a skeptic. Thankfully, we have many of people who have achieved great things, despite the evils of discrimination. There are well known examples, but there are many more that can be found in our local communities and our own families.

You have to believe in something outside of yourself to have a high level of positivity. There needs to be a spiritual, but not necessarily religious, component to this. People who believe good things will happen for them will start to become more perceptive of opportunities. They will also tend to attract those people who genuinely can help them.

There is a flip side to this type of thinking. If you truly believe good things are supposed to happen for you, then you will believe that if something doesn't happen, it just wasn't a good thing. I'll keep it real with you, sometimes this is a hard pill to swallow if you are in a desperate situation or have tried repeatedly at something. It's OK to feel disappointment, but we can't let it keep us down. Today, we have many opportunities to overcome our circumstances and do well. It can happen when we exude a faithful, positive mindset, with efforts to match!

SUMMARY: You must believe that it is your destiny to eventually come out on top. Skeptics will say that this is unrealistic, you're not facing the reality that bad things can happen. Not true!!! The skeptics are unrealistic; they aren't facing the reality that good things can happen! If you fail, you must have the attitude that it needed to happen for you to get to where you want to be. You must believe success is a birthright!

ACTION PLAN: Unfortunately, many of us have been conditioned to believe things aren't supposed to go our way. This can impact the amount and intensity of our efforts in pursuits of our aspirations. What are some strategies we can use to reprogram our minds for positivity?

Chapter 4

THE PRICE LIST

(YOUR EFFORTS)

My youngest daughter is a level 6 gymnast. She has been in gymnastics since the age of 3. As a result, I've had the opportunity to go to numerous competitions. If you've ever been to or witnessed gymnastics meet, you were probably amazed at the level of skill the gymnasts display to perform their routines. It is quite incredible. The athletes must remember the moves and perform them competently and safely. Gymnasts practice many hours a week, even at a young age. My daughter practices 3.5 hours a day, 6 days a week, as a level 6 gymnast, at 10 years old. This is in addition to having a full day of school. I admire her commitment for hanging with it.

At the end of every meet, as you likely already know, medals are given for 1st place, 2nd place, and so on. There are usually 10-20 gymnasts competing for medals based on skill level and age at typical gymnastics meet. The gymnasts receive placement medals for individual events and for overall scores. Because of the volume of participants, it is difficult to keep track of the placements until they are announced at the end.

I was attending a Level 4 meet for my daughter. I thought she had competed well and was anticipating the results. They started to announce the placements of the gymnasts, first place all the way to fifteenth place for the various events and categories. While they were announcing the placements, something occurred to me. In that moment, I realized that most of these young ladies were all very skilled and performed the events without any obvious flaws. They could all do the moves and skills. To the untrained eye, practically every gymnast would be touted as a future Olympian. However, there was 1st place, 2nd place, 3rd place, and so on. It was something small that separated each one from being that 1st place or 7th place finisher. Something that most of us would not even be able to recognize. We have all heard that you must put in work to be great; however, the visualization of seeing all of these very competent gymnasts being ranked really made me reflect upon that concept.

Around this time, I was asked by my principal to take on leading our campus's credit recovery program, which is called Achieve. Many teachers kind of frown on that position since you must deal with a lot of students who struggle for a variety of reasons. Many of the students are in Achieve for attendance and academic issues. Because of poor attendance, these students have struggled academically. There are a significant amount of students who have honestly made bad choices by not attending classes as required. Of course, if you aren't attending class, it is difficult to learn the material. Achieve is kind of the "last chance" for students that are short of credits. Many of these students are in danger of ultimately dropping out if they are unable to recover the credits. Achieve is basically a dropout prevention program. Achieve will be referenced on occasion throughout this book.

After taking over the program, one of the things I observed was a need for structure and motivation. The kids that are in Achieve struggle with motivation, even though it is their "last chance." As a result, I implemented structures to help them make progress. As far as motivation, I made posters of some of the mantras I believe in and try to live by. I made Achieve "Mr. Rodge's Neighborhood!" Now simply having posters on the wall does not make a classroom or program. I have seen classrooms that are wonderfully decorated with tons of inspirational posters but the students still "act the fool." I believe you must use those posters as a reference or discussion starter to truly add relevance. My daughter's gymnastics meet prompted me to create the following poster, which I reference in discussions with students in my classroom. It is my favorite.

Price List

Laziness $0

Talking/Empty Promises $1

Mediocrity $10

Being Good $80

* Being Great ** $100

You Have To Pay the Price!

I know, I know, it is not the greatest piece of artwork; that is by intention. But I love what it represents. And it really gets students to reflect. We always hear that there is a price to be paid for success, but what is that price? I figured if I could have money represent our efforts, that would make it much more concrete. Being lazy requires no effort. Laziness equates to doing nothing. It is easy to do nothing, but it won't get you anywhere. Talking and simply saying you are going to do something takes slightly more effort than being lazy, but it's still very minimal. We've all heard the saying "talk is cheap." Well, it is. Everyone can say they want a better life, more money, to be the best, to be health, etc. The list is endless. A person's word is worthless without action.

Let's ponder the value of talk some more by looking at strategies to get past simply talking about what we want. Talk is cheap! It really is. Think about it. It costs you hardly anything. It takes extremely minimal effort to do. Talk is important for communication, but the communication must be followed by action. How many things can be accomplished by simply saying that you are going to accomplish them? None come to mind right off the bat. What good is it to state you are committing to a healthier lifestyle if you do not exercise or eat healthier? What good does it do to state you need to quit _____ (smoking, drinking, spending money, etc.) if you choose not to change? We live in a world that respects action. Talk with no action undermines credibility. What follows are 3 strategies to make sure your "talk" is not cheap:

1. **Make yourself accountable:** Utilize formal and informal support systems if you struggle with being accountable. When we know we have someone to answer to, it helps us to fight through those times where our motivations may be a little low. Your support systems can include family, friends, groups, and social media networks. Documenting your actions or progress toward a certain goal on your social media account is an

excellent way of staying encouraged and accountable. Those who comment will likely be very supportive of you. Plus, you may unknowingly inspire someone. Allow it to be a positive tool.

2. **Change your people, places, or things:** Granted, in many cases, it is hard to make wholesale changes due to certain circumstances in our lives. However, we typically can change an aspect of our lives to some degree. For example, a person who is dieting may drink water or tea instead of soda. A person who is quitting smoking or drinking may avoid bars. The downside to this is that when we make changes to our people, places, and/or things, in many cases, those closest to us are the least supportive or understanding. A well-known verse in the Bible (Proverbs 27:17) states "As iron sharpens iron, so one person sharpens another." Whether you are a believer or not, one cannot deny the power, meaning, and truth behind this verse. An iron blade is best shaped and sharpened with another tool made of iron; most substances do not have the strength or durability to modify iron. In applying this principle to our lives, it is important for us to surround ourselves with people who are like-minded. The iron in our lives can be those that have similar goals and can provide genuine encouragement and

support with honesty. If we expect to reach our potential, we must surround ourselves with others who are striving to meet their potential. Those people will relate to what we are going through and are likely to provide needed advice and encouragement. We typically seek to be successful in several areas which are interrelated: relationships, financial security, spiritual growth, and work, to name a few. Striving for success in these areas is a complicated and difficult process with many potholes, stops, and detours along the way. No one achieves great success without the support of others. We all need and depend on others to provide support in some form or fashion. Support can be providing encouragement, advice, time, or financial support. The bottom line is that it is extremely important to surround ourselves with people who have similar visions and ideals like us. There is mutual benefit when we do this.

3. **Have a plan:** You want to have a plan in place for change. Your plan is your foundation. It will likely need to be adjusted; that is OK. Plans provide a vision. And it is always good to write down your plan or tell someone who will likely provide support and honest, but helpful feedback.

Next up on the price list is mediocrity. Mediocrity takes more effort than talking, but there really is not much that one must sacrifice to be mediocre.

As you can see, the price one must pay to be good at something is high. It takes effort and sacrifice to be good. For example, your 3.0 student must be organized and prepared for class. They likely must do some studying outside of class. There is a higher price to pay in effort in order to be good, yet there are some rewards for it.

Being great takes the most amount of effort. The price is high. Your 4.0 student has to sacrifice a lot in order to have that high average. They are studying while others are playing around online. They probably take meticulous notes. They may do extra research to better understand a concept they are struggling with. However, the efforts to be great tend to reap huge rewards. That 4.0 student likely receives large scholarships for college. They will likely be able to go to the college of their choice. The rewards make the price worth it.

An important caveat, which ties into my gymnastics story, is the difference between good and great. If you look at the price list, there isn't that much of a difference in price between good and great. It is usually something small that separate good from great. Just like the top finishers in the gymnastics meet I mentioned. All the gymnasts that placed in the top 10 can all do the same skills. They are all good gymnasts. But there is something small that the 1st place finisher is doing better than the 5th place finisher. It could be the assertiveness of movements, smiling, etc. It can be something very minor.

In summary, what can we learn from this? There is a price to pay to be good or great. Nothing good or great comes without sacrifice. If you want a healthy body, you will have to give up the comfort of sitting on the couch for an hour each day. If you want an education, you may need give up going out on the weekend so that you can study. It could be spending a few extra minutes on a task or exercise. It might be listening more instead of talking. Or it could be doing less of something, such as TV or social media. Small adjustments can pay huge dividends in terms of our results.

SUMMARY: We're all aware of the saying that nothing comes easy, but do we really believe it in our hearts? The more you want, the more you will have to sacrifice. I like to use our physical bodies as an example. Those of us that are the most fit dedicate a ton of effort to exercise, dieting, and positive habits compared to the general population. Fit people likely sacrifice time in bed or on the couch by going to work out; they also sacrifice the tastiest foods. However, they are rewarded with great health and admirable physiques. Bottom line, if you have high goals or aspirations, be ready to do what others are unwilling to do in order to attain them!

ACTION PLAN: What is it that you really want out of life within the next 2 years? What are you willing to sacrifice to make it happen? This is one way to determine if you have

passion for a particular aspiration.

Chapter 5

ASSEMBLY REQUIRED- THE TOOLBOX

(USING WHAT WE HAVE)

On Christmas day, I, like many parents, seem to always spend a significant portion of my day reading directions and putting together gifts which require assembly. It appears it is becoming more difficult to remove toys from packages and put things together. I swear, I think you need strength training to open some of these toy packages. Parents of young kids will know what I'm talking about. And let's not talk about having to put things together. I think all parents will soon need an engineering degree to put a lot of these toys together. OK, enough griping on my part.

My youngest daughter received a desk for a recent Christmas. I braced myself for the worst. I pulled out the instructions. I started to put the desk together. Surprisingly, the instructions were fairly easy to follow; but as anyone who has assembled furniture knows, it can be time consuming. The life of being a parent on Christmas, spending a portion of your day doing hard work!

The last step in assembling the desk was attaching it to a wall. The instructions recommended a specifically sized drill bit to drill holes and attach the desk. Of course, I did not have that size; I had a drill bit that was close to the recommended size. I knew I could not go out and purchase the recommended bit on Christmas Day. Even in this day and age, all the stores are actually closed on Christmas! I attempted a few alternatives, hoping they would work. I probably spent an hour or so trying different options, to no avail. After trying alternatives, without much more I could do, I decided to try the drill bit I had. It was not the size the instructions recommended, but it was close. Guess what? It worked just fine!

This situation is very symbolic of what happens daily. Many of us have wants, desires, and goals. We are often looking for ideal solutions to our goals, problems, etc. Many times, the ideal solution is not available. However, we often have what we need within our grasp! Especially in today's day and age, the right people, knowledge, and skills can be a few clicks of a mouse or taps on a smartphone away. Technology has connected our world and opened doors that were not available several years ago. We have incredible access to information nowadays, compared to when I was coming up back in the day. Finding information was so much more challenging back then. Now, the help we need to start our goals is at our fingertips from the comfort of wherever we are located.

I did not have the recommended or ideal tool for attaching the desk to the wall, but what I did have was good enough. We may not have the absolute, best resources for what we are looking to accomplish, but we usually have enough to get started. AND IT IS IMPORTANT TO SIMPLY START! Do what you can with what you have. I have seen so many instances where people are trying to put the "perfect" plan together. Because of this, it takes them forever to get started. Then, when they finally start, they encounter situations that they had not planned for. I guess my point is that it is much better to come up with a solid plan, not a perfect plan, and implement it. You are going to have to adjust along the way anyhow. Sports is a great example of this concept. A coach will create a game plan for a team. For example, a football coach may go into a game with strategy of wanting to pass the ball much of the game because he knows his opponent has a weak passing defense. However, come the day of the game, the weather may not make passing the ball a viable option. A good coach will adjust based on the situation at hand, despite what they planned for. We can apply this same principle to our lives.

Something else I want to touch on regarding the tools we have at our disposal is perception. How you see things is everything. There are some people who suffer through some truly horrific circumstances in their lives but are seemingly happy. Then, there are some who had a lot of things in their favor and are unhappy. Heck, I remember watching a program where the person acknowledged they had a great upbringing: loving & understanding parents, money, good schools, health, etc. However, can you believe they actually said that having that upbringing, one which seems to elude many of us, was a problem? Really??? Perfect example of how perception shapes our reality. If you choose to see something as a problem, it is a problem. To change our lives, it helps to change our perceptions. Below are 3 ways we can change our perception:

1. **Spend actual TIME helping people.** Notice I didn't say spend money to help people. Don't get me wrong, giving away money can be helpful, but it doesn't seem to provide the same sort of impact for the giver and receiver that spending time does. You will gain some insights into life when you spend time helping or getting to know someone. There are so many people out there who likely do not have what you have. The resources you have will become more evident and relevant.

2. **Read/Learn about people you admire.** Many times, these people have overcome great odds to achieve greatness. Their stories can be inspirational and, more importantly, provide perspective.

3. **Learn your history.** In addition to reading about history, talk to those who have lived through different eras. Understanding your place in a WORLDLY and HISTORICAL context will change your perception and put you on the path to finding your purpose.

We must use the tools that are available in our toolbox. This is a message which especially needs to be conveyed to all, especially our youth. Many come from challenging backgrounds, but there are people and resources that can put them on the road to overcoming their circumstances. The tools are usually available to at least get started. We must have the awareness to recognize and share available opportunities and start on the process of success!

SUMMARY: We probably don't have the ideal resources for reaching our aspirations, but we usually have enough to get from point A to point B or even C. The mistake so many people make when they are pursuing a goal is believing that everything should be perfect. WRONG!!! The best thing is to start; there will be so many unforeseen situations that you could have never predicted or thought to prepare for....... it's part of the process! That is how you learn and grow.

ACTION PLAN: What are some resources you have available

to you that you can use immediately to start on your path to success? Are there people who can offer support in the form of knowledge, and mentorship, without expecting something in return?

Chapter 6

Y.A.L.E.

(YOU ARE LEADERS EVERYDAY)

Anyone who has served any amount of time in the military knows that there is always constant change in the personnel of your unit. Coworkers, subordinates, and leaders are always coming and going to new assignments. You have the opportunity to work with so many different people with varying approaches to their work, even though the military is based on uniformity.

I served 5 years in the US Army as a mental health specialist, which is basically a counselor. During this time, I had an opportunity to work with a leader who has impacted me more than any other in terms of his approach to leadership. His name was SFC Eastman. He was assigned to take over (NCOIC for my military folks) the Behavioral Science department at the facility I was assigned. I was in my 20s' at the time and was learning a lot about how to function in the real world, being in a leadership position in the department myself.

I remember when SFC Eastman first took over. He was very deliberate in his actions. At the time, I thought he was too deliberate. He was very calm and reserved. He seemed too passive. He asked questions and took notes but didn't really jump into the functions of our department. As a twentysomething, it seemed kind of weird to me, to say the least. I thought leaders should come in, take charge, and immediately implement their program.

Boy was I wrong. After about a month or so, SFC Eastman had a meeting with us. He explained that he was observing how we operated and learning our strengths and weaknesses. He then explained how he planned to address areas we could improve upon. He also brought a level of organization to everything we did. It was more work for us; however, the changes were practical, thus everyone embraced the changes. He treated everyone respectfully and with equal importance. SFC Eastman was very firm in his expectations, but reasonable. His approach ultimately made our section much more productive and readied our soldiers for growth professionally. I learned a lot in my short time under SFC Eastman about leadership. He taught me that leaders should take time to be observant and learn all the facts, not to overreact or act in haste. You want to understand the "why" behind how things are functioning. You also want to take time to explain why there are changes, since it builds buy in and trust. SFC Eastman made a lasting impact on me.

I had to use many of the qualities that I learned from SFC Eastman when I took over the Achieve program at my campus. Anyone who has been assigned a new position in education after the beginning of the school year knows how challenging that can be. Students are already in routines; they don't take kindly to having to adapt to change.

I reflected upon my experiences in leadership. I knew I needed to take time to observe how the program was functioning, while fighting the temptation to make immediate changes. During that time, I had to do a quick needs assessment to prioritize what would get the students to be the most productive. I realized I could not address every issue immediately. I knew there would be some students who would be vocal about their displeasure with the changes, so I had to mentally prepare to deal with that in a way that would not further alienate the students. I chose to implement changes that would give the program "the most bang for the buck." As a result, the students' productivity significantly increased.

Whether you like it or not, we are all leaders. We are leaders of our families. We are leaders of a team on our job. We are leaders in our community. We are even leaders of ourselves. Even as a student with no position or authority, you are a leader. How is that? Because you have an ability to impact others.

I believe it would be great if we all carried ourselves with **exceptional** leadership qualities. I believe we would advance ourselves and others. Notice I said exceptional; I'm not talking about having the qualities of the dreaded bad boss. I'm talking about high quality leaders.

What qualities make great leaders? Leaders are faced with significant challenges, temptations, and responsibilities at any level. Aren't those the same obstacles that we face on a personal level? Essentially, if we can start to embody the qualities of great leadership, we can ultimately improve ourselves. Here are a few qualities I have observed and appreciate of effective leaders which we should embody on a personal level:

1. **Communication.** I'm sure that is a huge surprise, right? Seriously, we all need the ability to effectively communicate our needs and messages. Most people tend to think of communication as simply one's ability to deliver information. However, a large part of communication is the ability to receive and interpret information. Communication occurs verbally and non-verbally. Non-verbals are probably more significant than the actual words we speak. If our nonverbals (body language, expression, posture, etc.) don't align with our spoken words, the verbals instantly lose credibility. In being an effective communicator, you also must have the ability to determine the real meaning or purpose of communication. We all know of people who "beat around the bush" when attempting to make a point. Or they are not direct in

their communication because they don't want to be offensive. An effective leader will have an ability to listen and value input, regardless of person or position. Great insights can come from all directions. Communication is important for personal growth because we need to be able to listen to the sometimes-uncomfortable feedback we may receive as part of the success process.

2. **Vision.** A great leader can "rally the troops." In life, subordinates, and people in general, get so wrapped up in the day to day grind of living and working that we sometimes lose focus of the big picture. A great leader will put people in a position to maximize their contribution based on their abilities. As individuals, like leaders of an organization, we must identify our purpose regularly while being focused on the process.

3. **Prioritization.** Prioritization is related to vision. To prioritize is to understand what needs attention and what actions will yield the greatest positive impact. Prioritization is one of the most important duties of a leader, in my opinion. Most people tend to believe that whatever they are working on is of utmost importance to their group, team, family, etc.

Sometimes, there is truth to that but, in most cases, we tend to overestimate our importance. Don't get me wrong, what we do may be important, but not as much as we think. We all know of people who blow everything out of proportion. Everything is an emergency. Everything needs immediate attention. The sky is always falling. Great leaders can redirect. Through prioritization, a great leader can figure out what deserves immediate attention. Every situation does not require the same time and energy. We must use prioritization on a personal level also.

4. **Pragmatism.** I think pragmatism is such a neat word. I had not heard of the word (or at least was paying attention) until I heard a college instructor use it when I was working on my master's degree. Pragmatic is basically another way of saying practicality based on need. A leader must do what is practical, sometimes deviating from the ideal, in doing what is needed. Sometimes you find leaders and people who are so bound to a philosophy that they cannot deviate from it, even though staying put may mean obvious consequences. Good examples of pragmatism are found in the sports world. Great coaches can adjust their strategies to fit the players

the skills of the players they have on their team and/or to win a game. With pragmatism, there are certain things that are non-negotiables, like discipline and accountability. Whether leading your group or yourself, those qualities cannot and should not be sacrificed. In summary, we all must be insightful enough to adjust when necessary and do what needs to get done.

5. **Perspective.** Perspective kind of ties in with prioritization (see number 3). Great leaders do not overreact or make impulsive decisions. Leaders are the gatekeepers of the vision of an organization. When others may feel concern or start to panic, a great leader is able to take in all information, make a sound decision, and sell that decision to the people they lead. A great leader has the tendency to look at the upside of a situation, even if it is negative. They typically have a can-do attitude and emphasize overcoming the obstacles to be victorious in the end. We must have these qualities on an individual level. We must see the glass as half full. Your so-called realist will say that is not reality, you must call a spade a spade. Keeping a positive perspective does not mean you are ignoring the realities of a situation. It takes a positive perspective to

overcome negative situations. You must think you can do something in order to do it. If you don't think you can do something, chances are you won't be able to do it because you will lack effort or not even trying because of lack of belief. Perspective is important on a personal level.

6. **Consistency.** Slow and steady wins the race.... shouldn't the saying be nice and steady? Who really wants slow? Regardless, the idea behind that saying is the importance of being consistent. Many times, we tend to put a lot of energy into getting off to a fast start or finishing strong. Don't get me wrong, starting and especially finishing is extremely important. However, we all value consistency...the restaurant that regularly provides quality meals, the sports team that is always competitive, the cell phone with reliable reception, just to name a few examples. Who enjoys a team who wins 2 out of 10 games, even if the 2 victories are huge? Who wants to go to restaurant that gets the order right 1 out of 5 visits? Consistency doesn't mean perfection, because everything and everyone can come up short from time to time; but we should deliver to ourselves and others regularly. Take dieting for example. The person who maintains their diet 6 out

of 7 days each week is WAY more likely to lose weight than the person who fasts once a week. Here's another example of the value of consistency and balance. One day, two friends make a pledge to train for a marathon. Neither one is what you would consider to be a runner. Friend # 1 is a slacker; Friend # 2 is overly ambitious and does everything 100 mph. After 2 weeks, Friend # 1 has done absolutely nothing. Friend #2 has trained every day at peak intensity but is now in pain and has an injury. Overtraining is just as damaging as doing nothing at all. Let's apply what happened to the friends with our goals and ambitions. We do not want to be like Friend #1. We won't reach our goals if we just sit around and do nothing. We must take consistent action. As the saying goes, nothing changes if nothing changes. However, when we act, we must be careful not to overextend ourselves. "Doing the most" or doing too much, can be just as harmful. Our minds and spirits can wear down, just like our bodies, and impact our health, spirit, and relationships. Yes, it takes drive and energy to chase your dreams, but 100% on one day doesn't have to be the same 100% on another day. The best coaches structure their programs to vary in intensity. A team will not have super intense, draining practices every day. The most recognized organizations in our world today value work/life balance for their employees. Balance and consistency are keys to staying on the path to accomplishment. We must find balance in our lives, which will give us the long-term stamina we need for chasing our dreams and goals. Great leaders and great people are incredibly consistent to the point of being predictable. You must be capable of delivering to yourself and to others.

It is to our advantage to ourselves and those around us to conduct ourselves with the qualities that characterize effective leaders. The leader in you will lead you to the success you deserve!

SUMMARY: A leader is considered anyone who can have an influence or impact on others. Well, guess what? That means you! All of us are leaders. Leaders aren't solely based on authority, in fact, you do not need authority to be a leader. Leadership is about attitude, accountability, and initiative. When we begin to realize how we are potential role models for the people in our lives, we tend to carry ourselves and perform at a higher level.

ACTION PLAN: Think of someone you directly impact consistently. It can be a family member, friend, coworker, or

teammate. Why does that person admire and respect you? How can you make a positive impact on this person's life? By making a positive impact, how do you improve your own skills regarding your aspirations?

Mills Carnell Rodgers II

Chapter 7

3D SUCCESS

(WHAT SUCCESS ENTAILS)

I once heard a motivational speaker say, "You are going to fail your way to success." Kind of intimidating if you think about it, right? Hearing that might discourage some from even trying to chase their dreams. However, if your mind isn't conditioned to deal with disappointment to some degree, then it probably is not ready for the amount of trial and error needed to become successful. The reality is failure is not enjoyable, under any circumstances. Failure can be a great teacher but experiencing it just plain sucks! We need to be able to minimize our fear of failure when chasing our goals and dreams.

About a year or so ago, I decided to try my hand at e-commerce. Like any entrepreneur, I wanted to take more control of my destiny. I did my research and figured it was something that

I could do while I maintained employment to bring in some extra income. I decided to sell unused to gently used items from around the house on E-Bay and Amazon. They ended up selling quickly. It seemed like I was on to something. I started to research merchandise I could buy for wholesale at a reasonable price on a limited budget and sell for a profit on the e-commerce sites at a price that was competitive to retailers. Hmm, what could that be? Ties!!! They seemed like the perfect item. You can find decent quality ties at a low price from overseas and easily sale them at a price that was competitive with any retailer here in the United States. Plus, ties are easy to stock and cheap to ship. Brilliant idea, right?

Well, actually it was, but it came with some disclaimers. I did not consider the amount of competition there is on the e-commerce websites. The internet is a two-edged sword. Starting a business is so much more accessible than it was back in the day, which is great because so many more of us have the opportunity to live our dreams; however, the competition has skyrocketed because it is so easy to participate.

After a few months, with disappointing sales, I decided to stop actively pursuing the selling of ties on e-commerce sites. It wasn't worth it for me. I simply didn't have a passion for selling merchandise online, especially with the lack of success I experienced. There were too many things outside of my control regarding the marketing, algorithms, and that good stuff that comes into consideration when selling on the internet. I was motivated by the potential income it could provide, but that was not enough to drive me to keep actively pursuing that type of business. I can admit I failed at e-commerce. Sometimes, you must know when to let go. In all honesty, it wasn't something that I was super driven to do. I knew I wanted to do something to create my own income, but decided it wasn't e-commerce of that nature. It was very easy for me to walk away from. I did not feel a strong internal drive, in other words, passion, to continue. I realize every passion we have has "dirty work" involved, things we don't like to do. But I genuinely did not enjoy any aspect of it. I directed my energies toward something that had a greater relevance for me: coaching and speaking. BTW, I still have most of those ties!

The process of achieving success is filled with numerous challenges. It is easy to have a dream. Making it happen is a different story. Simply wanting is not enough. EVERYONE WANTS! What are you willing to do to get what you want? What are you willing to devote or give up in order to chase your goals or dreams? We must focus more on our process or plan toward our dreams as opposed to the dream itself. We must use the progress we make in our process as motivation.

As you have probably guessed, I like to come up with catchy ways to help us apply certain strategies, to help us stay motivated. Another concept I have created is 3D Success. Success is in 3D. Experiencing success depends on 3Ds:

- **Discipline**
- **Discernment/Decisions**
- **Desire**

First, let's talk about discipline first. I like to equate discipline to consistency. As mentioned earlier, progress in any area indicates positive, consistent actions toward an expectation or goal. We have a much greater likelihood of sticking with our goals if we are focused more on the consistent actions to reach a goal. Consistency in our actions leads to growing confidence, which strengthens our resolve in progressing toward our goals. To be successful, we must consistently make progress. Success doesn't happen overnight; it takes time. There will be trial and error along with disappointments. The road may have detours and delays, but you can reach your destination

Something important I feel that relates to being consistent is the myth of perfection. NOTIFICATION: YOU DO NOT HAVE TO BE PERFECT IN ORDER TO BE GREAT OR REACH YOUR GOAL! I think that is important to share because there are many times we quit or don't even try because we feel we're not perfect or have the perfect circumstances. Listen, we all make mistakes. Most of us have experienced deep disappointments, failures, or challenges. Luckily, we have opportunities to succeed in today's world despite this. Sports is a great analogy for understanding that we do not need to be perfect in order to win or be great.

Muhammad Ali is considered by many as the greatest boxer of all time; yet, he wasn't undefeated. He wasn't considered a power puncher. Despite this, he is still viewed as the best. The Houston Astros won the 2017 MLB World Series. They lost 61 times in the regular season. They experienced failure 61 times in the regular season yet were able to reach their goal of winning a championship.

Making the right decisions is also important. Unfortunately, there isn't a book of instructions for many of the situations we will encounter. Also, just because we have good intentions when we make decisions does not mean it is the right choice. Good intentions do excuse poor choices. That is why, especially as a young person, to seek out someone who can serve as a mentor. Of course, a mentor isn't going to know everything, but their insights can help. You can have mentors in a variety of areas in your life.

Lastly, you must have a strong desire to be successful. You must want it badly. Wanting it is what is going to keep you looking for answers when you are struggling. Sometimes I replace desire with desperate because you must want it bad, like your life depends on it!

I know there are some of you out there who have suffered some losses and abandoned your dreams. I am here to share some good news with you....... you are still on the path to accomplishing your goal! Thank goodness, each day allows an opportunity to resume! Remember, success is a process and not an event. In many cases, the process involves some stumbles, whether it is failure or losing focus. Many people who have achieved great success often had several stumbles, challenges, & failures along the way. So, celebrate the good news and be rejuvenated & refocused. This is your time to resume your progress on the path to accomplishing your goals. You got what it takes!! Examples abound of imperfect people making an impact and doing great things. Perfection is not needed on the road to success; you only need to stay on the road!

SUMMARY: There will be many challenges along the way. You will experience failure. Let's be real……failure does not feel good, even when a valuable lesson is learned. Sometimes we must try our hands at several things in order to figure out what is truly our passion. And like I previously mentioned in this book, don't seek perfection prior to getting started with your goals. Life is too short. Continuously seeking perfection will result in a loss of precious time. You will have a learning curve anyway, so you might as well start.

ACTION PLAN: Out of the 7 chapters of this book and their concepts, which one do you feel relates to your situation the most? Remember, success builds confidence and confidence can create more success. It's very important we find small ways to be successful to change our mindset so that we can live our dreams. YOU CAN WIN BEING YOU!!

ABOUT THE AUTHOR

Mills Carnell Rodgers is an author and speaker located in San Antonio, TX. He worked in schools with high at-risk populations throughout his 15 years as an educator. He is originally from Ville Platte, LA. As an educator, he has held positions to include special education teacher, general education science teacher, science instructional coach, academic instructional coach, administrative intern, Achieve coordinator, and substitute assistant principal. "Mr. Rodge" has also served in the US Army as a mental health specialist which, in civilian lingo, is a counselor. He is also a husband and a parent to his 2 daughters. His oldest daughter is diagnosed with moderate to severe autism. Mr. Rodge can honestly say that parenting a child with special needs has so many "behind the scenes" challenges that many people, including educators, overlook. He is compelled to share his insights about being parent to a special needs child with others in order to build awareness and ultimately improve how needs are met for at-risk students in general.

His personal and professional experiences have allowed him to gain some unique insights on a variety of topics that he believes can have a positive impact on the lives of many. Visit us at www.successisprocess.net to learn more.

Made in the USA
Monee, IL
18 August 2025

22496974R00036